Ashes to Ash

A 30-Day Devotional Journey
By Ashley Arendale Murphy

Introduction

As I sit here, in pain, writing poetry to God, I feel his presence in every part of it. I recently heard flowers grow in the valley.

My name is Ashley—you can all call me Ash—that's what my friends call me.

I spent 8 and a half years as a hopeless drug addict with nothing left, spiritually dead, and had no true relationship with my Heavenly Father. When my parents died 37 days apart, I was so mad at God.

Today, as I write you almost 8 years into a life saved by His grace, nurtured by His mighty hand—God carried me through.

I sit in my home & pour out my own personal psalms to God.

Today I'm a member of Hillview Baptist church, I attend any recovery group out there—I am all in.

And God uses me occasionally to tell my story of hope and redemption.

He is my fourth man in the fire & now as I sit recovering in a new life, fighting cancer, I know my God is still here.

He hasn't left me—He's fighting my battle with me. He gave me the story of Ezra to show me He's building something new & I also feel He wants me to write.

So welcome to a book filled with deep cries to God, deep gratitude,

some days faith of a mustard
seed.

A Prayer Over Who is Reading This Book

Father God, Jehovah Jireh, Yahweh,
I speak life, peace, stillness, Your presence.
I pray enemies flee and we call on the mighty name of God to rescue and give peace that surpasses all understanding.
May Your Spirit reign down over this reader right now, Father.
In the name of the Father, Son, and Holy Spirit,
You are the way, the truth, and the life.
You are with this person right now, Father.
Amen.

Dedication:

I want to dedicate this book to my amazing children—who despite my past have made a way for themselves:

To my son Tyler: I love you all the way to your heart, the rock & I am proud of who you became, the heart you have let people see it.

To my precious Carly: You are beautiful. Every part of what you have been through—God will use for a testimony.

To my precious Hayden: You are one of a kind, stay extra & be the light.

To all of you — you have the world at your feet and don't even know it. Trust God & know I'm always with you. I thank you for encouraging me, lifting me up, and being my rock. You all are my world.

I thank my husband for standing by me. I dedicate this devotion to you too. Thank you for being a warrior with me through this sickness & the unknown, for loving me & chasing God together.

Author's Note:

As you read these meditations, my wish is that you find grace and saving hope.

HOPE: Hold On, Pain Ends. And it really does—one day at a time, one moment at a time. One second at a time.

I pray you ask God to fill you with every ounce of what you need for whatever you are going through in this life.

I pray you feel—through these words—God has not forgotten you.

Grace be with you all. May God the Father comfort & protect you.

Yea, though I walk through the valley of the shadow of death, I will fear no evil, for my Father is with me.

Come to me all who are weary and heavy burdened, and I will give you rest.

Preface:

As you read each page of this book, I pray the Holy Spirit gives you eyes to see that you do not miss the mark set out before you; that you trust in every plan, in every valley, and every season. He is with you, molding you, building you, calling you for His purpose.

Pain is never something we ask for, but with each pain in this life, it calls us more towards growth, faith, and obedience. May these pages give you deep reflection into the growth of your own season. I pray you feel every word as if I wrote it with you on my mind.

The God of peace is with you; He is fighting the battle with you. May this be the 30-day hope shot, delivered and designed just for you. What you never knew you needed: every word, every heartache, every plead to God, and every tear came straight from my heart to these pages.

Why me? Why this season? But...Why not me?

God grows flowers in the valley, and I am so grateful; He plants the seeds. I tend more to the garden when I am in the valley. God pulls me out, and dead things come back to life. He does it every single time, even when faith wavers; He pulls me out.

I give all glory to Jehovah Jireh for writing through me, His precious daughter. I praise Him for awakening my soul and bringing these dry bones back to life, and to know that my Father lives, and He has not left me, not even for a second.

To a loving God that has pulled me out of the pit of hell, I praise Your name, Jesus Christ, Jehovah Jireh, Yahweh, Nissi, God of Angel Armies, Lord of Hosts, Prince of Peace, Jehovah Jireh, the Great I Am, the Beginning and the End, my Father, my Friend. May You reign forever and ever. May every page of this book be for Your glory, Father, that everyone may know Your name across the nation.

To my amazing mom — you were my person in this life. You leaving me here without you has been the hardest thing; the only peace I find with it is knowing you are dancing with the angels and knowing you loved Jesus and despised this world.

To my daddy — last time we spoke in my 13th rehab, you said, "You're going to do it this time, sweetie." You believed in me, and I did. I miss you; all your wishes for me came true.

To my brother Matt, who can be a pain in my side that I never would want to do this life without — thanks for being my biggest fan in every battle, good, bad, or ugly. I am always grateful that they left me with you.

To every friend in recovery —
thanks for proofreading, editing,
and being my cheerleaders. Y'all
are amazing, and I am so
honored by you all.

Acknowledgments

To every person that carried me through the journey of having cancer — first off, my boss **Shawn Burgamy**, for being a rock, soldier, and superhero all in one; my dear friend **Traci Bassie**, **Erin Jacobs** and husband **Randy**, her amazing, funny children; my aunt **Cindy McBride**, uncle **Tim**, her church, **Hill View Baptist Church**, **Jamie Bassie**, **Chris Bush**, **Crystal Bush**, **Will Conner**, **Scared Space**; every single employee of mine who even came to my house, cooked chicken, carried food, all of it, the pumpkins — I love you dearly.

Mississippi Delta Community College as a whole; every person who bought a chicken plate, the cards sent, **Karen and Keith**, all **Ben's brothers** who showed up for him in the waiting room; **Moorehead Garden Club** — **Brenda Grubb, Staci Janet** — Business Office at MDCC; **Tom King** — MDCC Bookstore; **Kelly & Melissa Evans** — and all **Sugar Plums guidance**; my friends **Jim, John, Kristen, Nicki, Ann, Carlos, Bob, Bryan, Barry & Patience**.

The **Emmaus Community**, every person who donated; **Ben's mom's church, Magee family**, and all the amazing cards; **MD Anderson Cancer Center** — all the amazing people who prayed over me and saved my life; **Dr. Graham & Dr. Artichoke Heartman** — I love you all. Dr. Graham, thanks for the new plastic surgery belly button and for slicing, dicing, and putting all organs back in place. **Camilo Jiminez, aka Dr. Artichoke Heart** — the diet saved my life, my soul, and I am so thankful for you.

Dr. Jerry, thanks for showing me your authentic self — I know you were God-sent. **Dr. Harper** from Carrollton and Carrollton Clinic, thanks for cutting through all the red tape and telling it like it was; you are the real MVP, and thanks for saving my life years ago from heroin and re-saving it from cancer.

My sponsor **Betty Woodcock**; my 99 friends in recovery all across the area — **Ricky Charlton, Pascagoula, MS**; again, my kids and husband — they were my biggest support and team: **Amanda Hicks, Arthur, Keirn, and Mitch; Rhonda Taylor; Pastor David and Sexy Sandy; Lori Beth; all my Hillview Church women; LO Sister Conference; Ben's mom Donna, who is my mom; my brother's mom Gayle McKnight; and my brother**.

To all the people not mentioned, I am so grateful for everything you did for me and my family. There just aren't enough words — I am overwhelmed at the goodness of God.

If it weren't for you all, and even the ones not mentioned, I would have seen the other side of this journey. Thank you from the bottom of my heart. You have shown me a love that I will continue to repay.

A Prayer for This Book

Jehovah Jireh, I pray this little book crosses nations.
May it make paths with people who need it most.

Father, I pray it reaches jails, institutions, rehabs, and homeless shelters.
I pray it reaches the broken, the lost, and shines hope into a dark world.

Father, I pray Your Holy Spirit will reign down.
I speak life right now over anyone touching or reading it.

Father, speak into their life.
Lord, let them know You.
Let them feel every word, every cry, and find hope in the pain.

Father, let this book be a light in the darkness.
Let it bring peace to the weary, courage to the afraid, and joy to the sorrowful.
Let it remind them that You are always with them, guiding, loving, and restoring.

Father, I pray hearts are opened and minds awakened.
Let every page be a seed of faith, every meditation a spark of encouragement.
May this book comfort the hurting, strengthen the weak, and uplift the hopeless.

Jehovah Jireh, I commit this work into Your hands.
Let it travel far and wide.
May it plant hope, build faith, and draw souls closer to You.

In Jesus' name, I pray. Amen.

Among the clouds, the waters,
and the deep sunshine I sat in
silence with my Savior to find a
new peace of mind.
To be still & know, I prayed You
to speak to me.
I humbly sat before Your throne
and asked You to open my eyes
so I could see.

As I turned the pages to the Bible
— Ezra — You revealed to me, the
temple was under construction.
It was a hard sentence to bear.

You built a temple in a city — it
was all underneath repair.
As they chipped & chiseled, You
were making something new.

That's when You spoke to me &
said: I'm doing the same thing in
you.

You said with a mighty whisper:
Do not be afraid, I am with you.
I heard You loud. You made sure
I knew.
You had called me by name.

I have left today with a newfound
peace.
For You are doing something
new inside of me.
I am Your temple & You will set
me free.
I am under construction — but
You're not done with me.

Day 1: The Lost Sheep

He leaves the one for the 99.

Great is Your faithfulness.

When You rejoice more over the one lost sheep that came back after being astray than You do for the 99 that never left, the kind of love that is!

You ate & walked and taught the ones who were counted out - the misfits, the prostitute, the tax collector.

When I think about it, I think about the same people we overlook today just like so many people did then.

The junkie, the alcoholic, the one who just doesn't fit in, the outcast, the bum in the store parking lot, the homeless guy begging for change, those are Your people too.

Why are we not showing the love we show to one another in church? The same love in the store parking lot?

Isn't that His child too? Wouldn't Jesus have walked with him? Wouldn't He have told the misfit girl, "Daughter, Your faith has healed You. Go in peace and be freed from Your suffering."?

Every time I read the Bible, it's telling me do not love the world. How easy it is to get caught in the worldly things! The devil's workshop has so many different avenues of attack.

Those same people aren't they the ones that God uses every single time?

That's the miracle! The proof through those same people who are counted out that He uses all for His good.

"For I know the plans I have for you," declares the Lord, "plans to prosper you and not to harm you, plans to give you hope and a future."

We don't know the plans so why do we count out that person so many times? We lose hope, declare failure. Can we not have FAITH OF A MUSTARD SEED?

Trust in the LORD with all your heart and lean not on your own understanding; in all your ways submit to him, and he will make your paths straight.

I could read that one every single day... He will move mountains but how easily do I forget when the answers are not coming. When what I wanted is not here already, when I can't see the way, when I don't understand the why.

Meditation:

God's love is vast and unending. He seeks the lost and celebrates when they return. Just as He cared for the outcasts in Jesus' time, He calls us to love those society often overlooks today. The faith that moves mountains is a mustard seed—a small yet mighty trust in God's perfect plan. When life feels confusing and the path is unclear, lean fully on Him. Submit your heart and surrender your worries, for He makes the way straight.

Scripture:

📖 **Jeremiah 29:11**

"For I know the plans I have for you," declares the Lord, "plans to prosper you and not to harm you, plans to give you hope and a future."

📖 **Proverbs 3:5-6**

"Trust in the Lord with all your heart and lean not on your own understanding; in all your ways submit to him, and he will make your paths straight."

Prayer:

Father,

Help me to trust You even when I don't understand. Strengthen my faith, so that I may be a light to those who feel lost or forgotten. Help me to carry with me a love for people the same way You have loved me. Open my eyes to the lost show me how to truly see them and show them the light of Christ. Teach me to love as You love, with grace and compassion.

Amen.

Day 2: Even In the Valley

Jesus, You're all that I need, my God.

Why do I run? Why do I flee?

Why does it take dark for me to say in my weakest moments I feel You most?

You are the root to my very soul.

I thirst and I thirst for You.

Why do I wait to the bitter end to seek the living water that resurrects me again and again?

You are the way, You are the life, so why does my flesh still fight?

I people-please again & again. No hope, all lost.

The world is not my friend. To go off like Jesus to that quiet place.

Why is so much pain what it takes, to seek Your peace to seek Your face?

In shame I run - that's not a part of the race.

Every time I feel I'm at my own demise I find Your grace never ends, a love that supplies.

Meditation:

In our weakest moments, God's strength shines the brightest. Though we often run or hide in shame, His love pursues us. The living water He offers restores and resurrects weary souls. Even when the flesh fights, and people-pleasing traps us, God's grace is unfailing. Seek Him quietly. In stillness, His peace envelops and renews.

Scripture:

📖 **2 Corinthians 12:9**

"My grace is sufficient for you, for my power is made perfect in weakness."

📖 **John 7:37-38**

"If any man thirst, let him come unto me and drink. He that believes in me, as the scripture has said, out of his belly shall flow rivers of living water"'

Prayer:

Lord Jesus,

In my weakness, be my strength.
Teach me to seek You first, to
find peace in Your presence, and
to rest in Your unending grace.
In the valley Father, I praise You
and trust You at my weakest
Father God, I feel You the most.
Amen

Day 3 He Is with You

My God, my Father, I felt Your peace, I see it over & over. You strengthen me with Your power divine.

Your strength unmatched. I can go through the war. ◉ My armor is in the Word. No weapon can match, although I may be under attack.

You're with me every step. I can feel You carrying me when I'm out of breath. When I have no peace and I'm in doubt, I continue to see You working it out. Serenity that can't be described – it's holy & it's from the divine.

You pour & You pour into me. When I stray, You keep planting seeds. This valley is deep, so I'll hold on to You. How beautiful it is to see You carry me through.

Your precious daughter loved so much & You continue to provide me with Your heavenly touch. I see Your grace, You're working it out.

I don't know the plan; I'll still lay it down, I surrender. I surrender, You set me free. My Father, My God, Your peace is all I need.

When the days are hard & I can't see through, You provide the way & I'm making it through. The valley is deep, but so is Your love. I feel it so close from heaven above.

Rabba, Teacher Jehovah, my Friend, I've seen You work miracles again & again. Even if not, I'll worship You still, I run the race for the prize at the end of this world. The win is mine to hear You say, "Well done my good & faithful servant". It'll all be worth it - I'll stand on my faith & to build Your kingdom day by day.

It won't be long and this will all fade away - a whisper, a wind, a test of faith.

My Father, My Father, I long for the day. I'll sing in glory, I'll dance, I'll praise!

Oh, for the day I see my Father's face - the sunlight of the Spirit, Your amazing grace.

Meditation:

God's peace is a fortress in every battle. Even when attacked or doubting, He carries us with a love that never fails. The valley may be deep, but His love is deeper still. Surrender your plans to Him; He is working it all out.

The race is long, but the victory is sure. Keep your eyes on the prize and your heart on the One who holds you. He has not let you go, Look up.

Scripture:

📖 **Ephesians 6:11**

"Put on the full armor of God, so that you can take your stand against the devil's schemes."

📖 **James 1:12**

"Blessed are those who persevere under trial, because, having stood the test, that person will receive the crown of life."

Prayer:

Father God,

Thank You for carrying me when I am weak. Help me to surrender daily and trust You fully. Give me strength to persevere and faith to see Your promises fulfilled. You are with me Father, God. You have the ultimate say, and You know the plan in every detail. You will work it all for my good. It's so beautiful to see You carry me. Teach me to rely on You, Father. The peace You provide surpasses all understanding, and I thank You for that peace right now, Father.

Amen.

Day 4 I Will Abide

ABBA

I know You are near, but my Lord, my God, I can't see You through all the fear.

The pain is numb; I can't seem to feel. Every part of this season just feels surreal.

I know You prune me so I can grow. If I am the branch, I feel I'm withering slow. You are the vine, let me take up my shield.

I long for the umbrella that protects me from the pain. I need Your grace to even make it through a day.

This must be the desert & I am in the season of drought. My God, my God don't forsake me now.

The living water is the only thing that can see me through. I am completely lost without You.

You are my God, the fortress on which I stand. How dare I be down here with my demands?

The harvest is plentiful, and I know this will reap its rewards. The God who multiplies also restores.

Yea, though I walk through the valley of the shadow of death, my Father is with me every step.

If it's disconnection in the line, it's never You that severed the tie.

You are the branch & I am the vine. You are the umbrella & always on time.

When the season may seem dry, I'll trust in the harvest. You planted the seeds just right - always in line.

You knew before what would happen now. You've already made a way I have no doubt. Your plans are good, Your ways are high.

The God who strengthens me is by my side. Even when I question, even when I doubt, I see Your word, You will work it all out. It'll be better than I've ever seen.

You're watering seeds cause You're moving me. I asked and asked, "What was Your plan?".

I told You to shake it up for grand. I told You I wanted to sell out my soul, to lay down my life & now look what unfolds!

You're building a foundation in all this pain. You're watering seeds, You created the rain.

Meditation:

In the dry seasons of life, God is still present, pruning and preparing us to grow. Though pain and numbness may cloud our vision, His strength is our fortress. Trust that He is working all things for good, planting seeds that will bear fruit in His perfect timing. Even when doubt creeps in, hold fast to His promises.

Scripture:

📖 **John 15:5**

"I am the vine; you are the branches. If you remain in me and I in you, you will bear much fruit; apart from Me you can do nothing."

📖 **James 1:2-3**

"Consider it pure joy, my brothers and sisters, whenever you face trials of many kinds, because you know that the testing of your faith produces perseverance."

Prayer:

Lord, when I feel dry and distant, remind me You are near. Strengthen my faith, help me trust Your plan, and nurture the seeds You have planted in me. You are preparing the way Father God, prepare me in this season. God grow me, I want to seek You above all else. You are the way, the truth and life. I praise Your holy name, and I thank You for what I don't see yet. I thank You, Lord, I know it's good. I know You prepared it for me. The harvest is plentiful, grow me in this season. Prepare me for that harvest God, for the crops will be plentiful. Amen.

Day 5 Holy Spirit Come

I believe in Your Holy Spirit.

I believe in the healing power of You, Jehovah, Prince of peace - the one over the angels, the messengers, the winds, and the fire.

I believe You heal and restore.

I believe You work it out for my good.

I believe Jesus died so the Holy Spirit can live in me & save me from my sins.

I believe You are moving.

I believe You're a faithful God, a just God, a God of grace.

You are the good shepherd for Your sheep.

You leave the 99 for me.

You chased me down.

You are a good Father.

You are the living water.

You are the thirst in dry land.

You are good and You know all plans.

You've seen the bigger picture, better yet, You created it.

You've sent people my way.

You already defeated the battle.

You are the fourth man in the fire.

You're the peace that doesn't make sense.

You are working it for my good.

You will be glorified - I will believe.

Meditation:

Faith in the Holy Spirit brings healing, restoration, and peace beyond understanding. God's plans are perfect, and He is always working behind the scenes for our good. Remember, Jesus is our Good Shepherd who leaves the ninety-nine to find the one. We can rest in the assurance that God's presence never leaves us, even in the fire.

Scripture:

📖 **John 14:26**

"But the Advocate, the Holy Spirit, whom the Father will send in my name, will teach you all things and will remind you of everything I have said to you."

📖 **Psalm 23:1**

"The Lord is my shepherd, I lack nothing."

Prayer:

Holy Spirit,

Fill me with Your presence. Heal my heart, guide my steps, and give me peace. Help me to trust in God's perfect plan and to walk boldly in faith.

Amen.

Day 6 When Faith Feels Small. Will You Run the Race Set Before You?

The faith of Moses, David, Saul & Noah, hard pressed on every side, but they didn't give up. We run the race set out for us with perseverance. We will suffer but we run the race for the prize. You're telling me to keep my faith but I feel like I have none.

Where is Your presence? Why have You forsaken me? Oh God, where is the peace when You showed me Ezra? Where are You in the suffering? What is the plan? What are You changing? Why do I feel so numb, so lost, without peace?

I know I am reading Your word. I'm doing the plans, but I'm not trusting. I'm not seeking in silence. I'm not praying wholeheartedly. I want to give up, to hide in a hole, to crawl into nothingness.

I will seek You & I will run the race. I will greet strangers and try to love the way You loved people. I can do more with the people in prison & I can step out more.

I have chased money, but I don't know what You want me to do. I will seek out the faith & relationships for You to move into my life.

I know You said You will never leave or forsake me. I still feel forsaken. Jesus suffered and died for me.

Is my faith in my head & not my heart? I don't feel I am living up to the calling.

Is this about obedience? Are You equipping me for something bigger and I just can't see it right now?

I know the plans I have for you - plans to prosper you and not to harm you, to give you hope and a future.

Meditation:

Even the strongest believers— like Moses, David, and Noah— faced deep uncertainty. You are not alone in asking "Where are You, God?" Your honesty is not a failure—it is the first step in returning to deeper faith. In the silence, God is equipping you. In the confusion, He is training your obedience. Keep running the race. Even mustard seed faith moves mountains.

Scripture:

📖 **2 Corinthians 4:8**

"We are hard pressed on every side but not crushed; perplexed, but not in despair."

📖 **1 Thessalonians 5:24**

"The one who calls you is faithful, and he will do it."

Prayer:

Lord,

I feel tired and unsure. But I'm still running. Help my unbelief. Strengthen the places in me where trust has thinned. Use every weakness as space for Your glory. Help me praise You in every storm and worship You in every way. Father, may this prayer come with a thankful heart. Help me be all You called me to be. Help the light You gifted me shine even in the darkest moments. Let the spirit lead me father. Yahweh, I know You are near. Amen.

Day 7 – Where You Are, Peace Follows -

Father God, the peace I feel, the miracles I see—it's just unreal.

Where You are near, the devil will flee.

My God, my Father, You must be right next to me.

I feel Your words; You fill my soul, nothing but the Holy Ghost.

My wounds are deep, but so is Your love.

You paved the way from heaven above.

My faith still stands; You strengthen my hope.

Jesus, You are near—don't let me go.

Meditation:

Today, let these words remind you that God's presence is powerful and real. Even in your deepest pain, His peace can overwhelm it. His nearness is your protection, His Spirit, your comfort, and His love you're healing. Today bask in the gratitude of what has already been restored in your life, find gratitude in all God has already changed, that you have already overcome, he's not even finished.

Journal Prompt:

- When have I felt God's presence the most strongly?

- In what area of my life do I need to be reminded that He is near and the enemy must flee?
- Write a short prayer or gratitude list using your own words.

Scripture:

📖 **Psalm 34:18 (ESV)**

"The Lord is near to the brokenhearted and saves the crushed in spirit."

Prayer:

Father,

Thank You for being so near that I can feel Your peace when chaos surrounds me. Thank You for filling my soul when I feel empty and for pushing back darkness when it tries to consume me. I know my wounds run deep, but so does Your love—and that love heals. Help me hold onto You tightly. Strengthen my hope, increase my faith, and never let me go. You are the Messiah, The Great I am, The Healer.

In Jesus' name, amen.

Day 8 Give Him Thanks, Praise Even in the Hardships

And I will give You thanks all the days of my life

even in the sorrow, Father God, I will call out to You

even in the questioning, the sadness, the pain.

My bones ache & my body longs for rest,

only You satisfy my thirst.

I find myself alone in dry land,

dry bones come back to life,

the world snares and traps and clings,

let me let go, Father God,

You are my only peace

all that I will ever need,

You lead me beside still waters

and You restore my soul,

How long must I linger in this
land

A citizen of nothing without You,
Father?

How long must I suffer?

Weeping may come, Father

but joy cometh in the morning,

and I will praise my Father

all the days of my life

I will dwell with You in the
kingdom

& give thanks to the heavens

for Your strength never fails

and Your love lasts for eternity,

shouts to You of praise

You will bring me through

hosanna to the highest King forever.

Meditation:

Be still in the presence God.

Let your spirit breathe in peace and exhale every burden.

Feel the dry places begin to soften in His presence.

Feel the sunlight of the spirit, who the Son sets free is free indeed.

Let your heart settle beside still waters.

This too shall pass, this ache won't be forever.

The heaviness will lift.

The Lord is near to the broken hearted and saves those crushed in spirit.

He restores.

He sustains.

He brings joy in the morning.

Scripture:

📖 **Psalm 30:5**

"Weeping may endure for a night, but joy comes in the morning."

📖 **Ezekiel 37:4-5**

"Prophesy to these dry bones, and say to them, 'Dry bones, hear the word of the Lord! I will make breath enter you, and you will come to life.'"

📖 **Psalm 23:2-3**

"He makes me lie down in green pastures; He leads me beside still waters. He restores my soul."

Prayer:

Father God,

In my weakness, be my strength. In the silence, be my song. I lift my heart to You—even in the ache, even in the questioning. Breathe life into these dry bones and into these dry places in my life Father God. Restore my soul. Let Your joy rise like the sun. Hear my praises in the pain, Father. I trust You to bring me through. Hosanna to the highest King forever.

Amen

Day 9- My Rescue Story

Heavenly Father
You give me a peace
over and over
You rescue me,
I run to Your Word,
so secure,
resting on Your promises
in You I can endure,
run the race,
be bold in my faith,
In my own strength
no more I can take,
but with You I press on
I run with the endurance
of Your love
I run for a prize
not here
in heaven above.

Meditation:

There is a kind of peace that only God can give—the kind that settles the soul even in the middle of the storm. When our strength is gone and we feel like we can't take another step, His promises become our anchor. His Word is a refuge; His love is the fuel that helps us keep pushing forward. We are not running for earthly prizes or applause, but for a heavenly reward. Endurance in faith isn't about perfection, it's about obedience; it's about trusting Him to carry us through.

Scripture:

📖 **2 Timothy 4:7–8 (ESV)**

"I have fought the good fight, I have finished the race, I have kept the faith. Henceforth there is laid up for me the crown of righteousness, which the Lord, the righteous judge, will award to me on that day..."

Prayer:

Lord,
You are my rescue and my rest.
When life weighs heavy and I feel
too weak to move forward,
remind me to turn to Your Word.
Help me not to lean on my own
strength, but on the truth of who
You are. Let me run this race
with bold faith, with eyes fixed
not on what I see, but on what
You've promised. Strengthen my
spirit with endurance &
obedience for Your plan Father
and set my heart on heaven.
In Jesus' name,
Amen.

Day 10 The Unknown

The Unknown this faith-shaking
place
the fear and dwelling in the
doubt
in that part of my pity
I can't find peace
Nothing makes sense
 I am far beyond figuring it out,
The way, the truth, the life
It's in Your Word
and You tell me to fight,
to be still
to rest,
to have faith,
baby steps,
You're making something new,
I can hear Your voice in the
suffering
more than I even knew,
all the days of pain, fear & doubt,

one simple word from God
You work it out
it's all gone now,
to walk away & seek You in the
still
I find You in the quiet,
I know I always will.
You've let me know
You're with me in the valley
Looking down
watching me grow,
Your beautiful daughter
an orphan no more
my Heavenly Father
A part of His grand design
the finale not yet arrived
the plan so unknown,
my mind couldn't fathom
the miracles You produce,
no dry bones can make fruit,
be the salt
be the light.

Another day
another fight,
My Lord, my Father
by my side,
You have anointed me with oil
& my cup it overflows, still
waters run deep laying it all at
Your feet.

Meditation:

There's a place in our journey where the unknown shakes our faith to the very core, and fear whispers louder than hope. But even in the rock bottom, God is present. In the stillness, in the valley, in the doubt—we are not alone. He defines us & builds character through our suffering and whispers direction in our waiting. What feels like the end is only the beginning of something new. Stay obedient, Our Father doesn't leave us alone; He gently teaches us to trust Him step by step. He calls us to be salt and light, even while we're still healing. And even in our weakest moments, He equips us, reminding us that we are His.

He doesn't call the equipped he equips the called.

Scripture:

📖 **Psalm 23:5–6 (NKJV)**

"You anoint my head with oil;
My cup runs over.
Surely goodness and mercy shall
follow me
All the days of my life;
And I will dwell in the house of
the Lord
Forever."

Prayer:

Father,
I don't always understand the
path, and sometimes the weight
of the unknown feels too much to
carry. But You are the God who
sees me in the valley. You carry
me, I am not alone, not an
orphan, not abandoned. You
anoint me with Your presence,
and Your Spirit overflows in me.
Lord, help me find You in the
still, hear You in the quiet, and
trust You even when nothing
makes sense. Make me salt and
light. Give me courage to take the
next step & gratitude for what I
can't even see that I know You're
working for my good. Thank You
for calling me Your daughter.
In Jesus' name,
Amen.

Day 11 Painted Promises

Father God,
I've been in such despair
looking up
feeling You nowhere,
where I'm at
wasn't even in my plans
but every ounce of my being
felt You
when my feet hit the sand,
the sky purple
the water so blue,
surrounded by the love
You knew I needed
by me too,
A wave crashed
A memory in the wind
sitting under the heavens
thinking of Your majestic plans,
I felt my soul

come back to life
as You had painted
the most beautiful paradise,
I know You're watching us,
It's a hell of a view,
my son beside me
the sky fading slow
Your promise painted in it,
I can finally let go.

Meditation:

Sometimes peace comes not in
the absence of fear, but in the
middle of it—in the moment you
stop fighting, just long enough to
breathe & be still. God meets us
there. At the water's edge. In the
hush of sunset. In the presence of
someone we love. He writes
healing into the sky and whispers

courage into the wind. And somehow, in the thick of madness uncertainty, and pain... you feel Him. The pain doesn't win. He paints His promise right in front of your eyes, your soul knows: He's carrying you, you can finally let go, because He's got it all.

Scripture:

📖 **Isaiah 26:3 (NLT)**

"You will keep in perfect peace all who trust in You, all whose thoughts are fixed on You!"

Prayer:

Father,
I didn't expect to meet You like this—but You knew I needed this moment. You quieted the noise. You reminded me that You're still painting beauty in my story, even in the unknown. Thank You for being with me in the middle of the pain. For showing up in the wind, in the waves, in the presence of my son. Lord, I give it all back to You. Hold me through what's next. I trust You. I let go.
In Jesus' name,
Amen.

Day 12 – Dead Things Come Alive

The chief of sinners,
I feel Paul's every word,
& I feel not worthy of You, Lord.
It says You are close to the
broken hearted
and those crushed in spirit,
I feel crushed on every single
side,
my God please restore me.
I know You can bring dead things
back to life,
Your Word says You bless those
who are spiritually poor,
& God, I feel poor to my very
core,
& I just keep trusting
You're the God who gives back
more,
My bones ache

I prayed like David
for You to bring back the joy,
To not forget how far You've
brought me now,
to be humble
You'll work it all out.
the God who multiplies
the God who supplies,
the God who raised Lazarus
Back to life.

Meditation:

Sometimes the most sacred
prayers are the desperate ones—
whispered between pain and
hope. When you're emptied out
and aching, God doesn't ask you
to pretend. He draws near.
You're not too broken for Him.
He sees spiritual poverty, the

crushed spirit, and He calls it blessed. Like David, you can pray for joy to return. Like Paul, you can confess your weakness and still stand in grace. And like Lazarus, your story isn't over. God is still the God who restores what looks dead. Even in ashes, He is writing resurrection.

Scripture:

📖 Psalm 34:18 (ESV)

"The Lord is near to the brokenhearted and saves the crushed in spirit."

📖 Psalm 51:12 (NIV)

"Restore to me the joy of your salvation and grant me a willing spirit, to sustain me."

📖 **John 11:25 (NLT)**

"I am the resurrection and the life. Anyone who believes in me will live, even after dying."

Prayer:

Father,
I come to You poor in spirit,
crushed in ways I can't explain. I
feel the weight of my sins, my
fears, my weariness. But I know
You are near. I trust You to
restore what's broken. I trust You
to bring back joy. Thank You for
grace, for not leaving me where I
am. You are the God who
multiplies my little and supplies
what I lack. You are the God who
brings life out of death. Raise up
what has been lost in me, and let
me walk forward in humility,
hope, and healing.
In Jesus' name,
Amen.

Day 13 Ashes to Ash

My Father,
this battle in my mind
It's continuing to haunt me
time after time,
I hear Your word
Be still & know,
some days I'm being still
with absolutely no hope,
the flesh is piercing
& it's as if it's winning,
not on Your Word
I don't feel Your rest
& lately every day
feels like a test,
Is this the enemy's schemes,
I think he's fully after me,
all this time in my mind
playing back every moment
line after line,
in the future

in the past
not leaning on You,
not staying in today,
falling short
reading Your Word
knowing it's sharper
than any two-edged sword,
the days keep moving forward,
& I ain't put my faith in You,
Lord.
What I did yesterday
won't keep me spiritually clean
today
Father God, please lead the way,
my faith won't fail,
You control the outcome
of the wind, fire & rain,
the armor in You,
my God never moves,
I may fall
I may stray
but You, my God

are still with me all my days,
until the end of the age,
working it out
loving me gracefully
when I still count You out,
The God of the angels,
You work it all out
in Your will
in Your time
I could go on
rhyme after rhyme,
The beautiful love
You left the 99
to go find the one
& how You sent Your one and
only Son
to save us
From our own mistakes,
My pains so deep
I have to bring it to You for grace
my Father, my God
I've watched You move

I've seen You do it
and You'll do it again
I just have to be honest
and say
This feels like it'll never end
I know I can look back
and see the other side
how You brought me through
every single time
gave ten-fold
what it once was
my God, my Lord,
You restore.
& when I think it's over
and I don't see the hope
my Father, my God,
You rise the sun
& I can see the light,
the process was hard to bear,
but You never left me
through the night,
I'll say with a whisper

Jesus
wrap me in Your loving arms
& then I always knew
it gets darkest
before the dawn

Meditation:

The mind is often the fiercest
battlefield. We fight fear, shame,
memories, doubts—and the
enemy knows exactly how to stir
it all up. But even in that swirl of
darkness, your whisper reaches
heaven. When we feel we've
fallen too far, wandered too long,
or failed too many times, God
doesn't move. His grace stays.
He's the God of restoration, of
second chances, of sunrise after
the night. We may wrestle with
our thoughts and stumble in our

walk, but His love remains. He is faithful even when we're faint. And though it may feel like it'll never end, He's already at work bringing light.

Scripture:

📖 **2 Corinthians 10:5 (NIV)**

"We take captive every thought to make it obedient to Christ."

📖 **Romans 8:38–39 (NLT)**

"And I am convinced that nothing can ever separate us from God's love. Neither death nor life, neither angels nor demons, neither our fears for

today nor our worries about tomorrow..."

📖 Hebrews 13:5 (ESV)

"I will never leave you nor forsake you."

Prayer:

Jesus,
My mind is a storm some days—racing, doubting, hurting. But I come to You honestly, just as I am. I confess that I haven't always trusted You, haven't always stayed in today, but You haven't left me. You are still God. You are still good. Wrap me in Your arms again. Help me take every thought captive and speak truth over the lies. I thank You

for being the God who restores,
who walks through the valley
with me, and who brings light
every time I think it's over. I'm
holding on to You, my Rock, my
Father, my Peace.
In Jesus' name, Amen.

Day 14: I AM WHO I AM

Poem

ABBA, Father, Jehovah, my Friend

I've seen You work miracles again & again,

this time I didn't think I would make it through the pain,

but You're the God who sends sunshine after the rain.

Tomorrow is over, I run a new race,

I march, I will not stray,

I want what You have in store for me,

You are the God that parts the Red Sea,

Your will not my way,

Father, help me stay in the faith.

Meditation:

Life often brings us to the end of ourselves—moments where it feels like nothing, but ashes remain. Yet God specializes in bringing beauty from ashes, hope from despair, and light from the darkest storms. The poem reminds us that even when we think we cannot endure, God sends His sunshine after the rain. He calls us not to give up, but to rise, step up, and keep our eyes on the faith that sustains us. Staying in the faith means surrendering our will for His, trusting that His plan is greater than our pain.

Scripture:

📖 **Isaiah 61:1-3 (KJV)**

"To appoint unto them that mourn in Zion, to give unto them beauty for ashes, the oil of joy for mourning, the garment of praise for the spirit of heaviness; that they might be called trees of righteousness, the planting of the Lord, that He might be glorified."

Prayer:

Father,

Thank You for taking ash and trading it for beauty. Even in my weakness and pain, You remind me that You are the God who parts seas, lifts the heaviest weights, and restores happiness joy and peace. Teach me to stay on the mark, to run with endurance, and to trust Your way above my own. Help me to see the sunshine after the rain and to walk boldly knowing You are with me.

In Your loving name, Jesus,

Amen.

Day 15 He Has Called You by Name

Your grace is enough
I want to drown in Your love
You came before
You already knew
Lord, I was called for You
No need to be afraid
You called me by my name
Nothing shall come before
You heal & restore
Your grace is enough
Surround us with Your love

Meditation:

There is a peace that doesn't depend on circumstances—only on presence. His presence. The kind that holds you when life feels like it's falling apart. The kind that walked ahead of you before you ever arrived at your breaking point. His grace goes before, surrounds, and remains. You don't have to strive to be seen. You are already known. Already called. Already loved. He will fill the gaps and overflow the void. His grace truly is enough— for every fear, failure, and moment when you didn't know how to take the next step. You were never meant to carry it alone. Let go. Let God. Let grace carry you. Sometimes we must wave the white flag of surrender to win.

Scripture:

📖 **2 Corinthians 12:9 (NIV)**

"But he said to me, 'My grace is sufficient for you, for my power is made perfect in weakness.' Therefore, I will boast all the more gladly about my weaknesses, so that Christ's power may rest on me."

📖 **Isaiah 43:1 (ESV)**

"Fear not, for I have redeemed you; I have called you by name, you are mine."

📖 **Psalm 23:6 (NKJV)**

"Surely goodness and mercy shall follow me all the days of my life; and I will dwell in the house of the Lord forever."

Prayer:

God,
Remind me that I don't have to be everything—You already are. When I feel lost, spiritually exhausted, or not good enough, anchor me in the truth that Your grace is sufficient. Thank You for going before me, for calling me by name, and for never letting me walk alone in anything. Let Your love quiet every fear and fill every hole in my heart. Give me Your eyes to see I cannot mess it up. Wrap me in Your loving arms, restore what has been

broken, and bring dry bones back to life. I trust that even in this—especially in this—You are enough & when I cannot walk Father, You will carry me. Amen.

Day 16 – He Heals the Sick

When I fall, let me fall to You
When I praise, let it be for You
Lord, when I rise, let me kneel
for You
God, when I speak, use me to say
things I never knew
When I run, I want to run to You
When I hit my knees, let it be to
You I'm hitting them too
You offer a love I never knew
Mercy that never fails, grace we
can't run through
You take the darkest time and
make us brand new
All the bad we used to do—
Still, we're saved by You

Meditation:

There are moments when we feel completely defeated—worn out by the chaos of this life. But God never leaves us in those moments. He's not just present; He's pursuing. His love doesn't wait for us to have it all together. It meets us in the fall, holds us through the run, and lifts us when we kneel. This journey isn't about perfection; it's about presence—His. Grace is not just something God gives—it's who He is. And He's already written redemption over every part of your story.

Scripture:

📖 **Psalm 139:7-10**

"Where can I go from Your Spirit? Where can I flee from Your presence? If I go up to the heavens, You are there; if I make my bed in the depths, You are there... even there Your hand will guide me, Your right hand will hold me fast."

📖 **Micah 7:18-19**

"Who is a God like You, who pardons sin and forgives the transgression of the remnant of his inheritance? You do not stay angry forever but delight to show mercy. You will again have compassion on us."

📖 Romans 8:1

"Therefore, there is now no condemnation for those who are in Christ Jesus."

Prayer:

God,
When I fall, catch me. When I rise, keep me anchored in Your Holy Spirit. Let my words be shaped by heaven, and my life point back to Jesus. Take the places in me that feel too far gone, too dark, or too hopeless— and remind me nothing is beyond Your reach. Let Your love flood every moment. Use my story, even the parts I used to be shameful about, for Your glory. I don't want to run anywhere

else—I want to run to You. Thank You for saving me even when I thought I was beyond repair. Thank You for loving me even when I ran from Your open arms. Amen.

Day 17 - Orchestrated Before You Knew

Your love is peace, strength, and everything in between.
You came before You already knew
Yet I still was living in fear, not trusting You.
I lean on Your Word; You surround me with ease.
I'm so proud I'm Your daughter, so grateful to be free.
You saved me in my darkest hour — I hit my knees.
You already knew. You were here before.
And I know I can count on You forevermore.
My Father, My Savior, Jesus Christ, My Lord.

Meditation:

There is something deeply comforting about knowing that God has already walked into our tomorrow. He is not pacing heaven in confusion or surprise — He *already knew*. This poem is a testimony of trust rediscovered, of fear being silenced by His unwavering love.

Even when we hesitate, when we hold on to fear, He surrounds us with peace. The beauty here is not just that He saves — it's that He was there before we ever cried out. He knew our dark hour. And yet, in His mercy, He still came to rescue.

Today, let's meditate on what it means to truly trust a God who goes before — who knows the outcome when we don't, who offers grace when we stumble, and who never walks away.

Scripture:

📖 **Deuteronomy 31:8 (NIV)**

"The Lord himself goes before you and will be with you; he will never leave you nor forsake you. Do not be afraid; do not be discouraged."

📖 **Psalm 139:5-6 (ESV)**

"You hem me in, behind and before, and lay Your hand upon me. Such knowledge is too

wonderful for me; it is high; I
cannot attain it."

Prayer:

Father,
Thank You for always going
before me.
You are already in my tomorrow.
When fear tries to take over my
heart, remind me that You've
already paved the way.
When I can't see the plan, help
me lean into Your peace and have
faith You will work it for my good
every single time.
No matter what it looks like, if
it's in chaos & shambles, You
bring beauty from these things.
Father in heaven, You have a
plan.

Like Job said, Father, the Lord
gives and takes away, blessed be
You, Lord.
Help me find strength in the
weakness; help me hold on a
little longer God.
Thank You for saving me —
repeatedly — even when I
struggle to hand it over and trust
You.
I'm so honored to be Your
precious child.
Cover me in Your grace, wrap me
in Your strength,
and remind me moment by
moment I can always count on
You.
My Savior, My Redeemer, Holy
One, Everlasting Father, King of
all Kings.
In Your loving name,
Amen.

Day 18 – Trust the Testing

Be the salt. Be the light. Be bold.
Stand in the faith. Be the
example. Live right.

Grass will wither. Flowers will
fade.
I'll hold you near.

Call upon My name — I will lift
you up.
Perseverance produces
character.

I, the Father, am building you
up.
Stay obedient in the race.

I, your Father, will soon see your
face.
My good and faithful servant —
well done indeed.

A heavenly home, by My throne you'll be.

The rewards you've gained, the pain you bore,
Will all have purpose — to this Man upstairs.

I will mold you and build you,
Do something new.

Just remember, child — have faith.
Trust the testing.

I am working on you.

Meditation:

Sometimes we wonder if our obedience is noticed. We stand firm, live right, and walk the hard path — and yet the pain lingers;

the reward feels distant, and the testing keeps coming. But this poem reminds us: *God sees.* He is not just watching you struggle — He is *building you through it.* When life feels dry and everything else fades like withering grass, He remains. His process is molding you, not breaking you. Trust the testing. It's not punishment. It's preparation. Every faithful act, every tear you've sown, is growing something eternal.

Scripture:

📖 **James 1:2-4 (NIV)**

"Consider it pure joy, my brothers, and sisters, whenever

you face trials of many kinds, because you know that the testing of your faith produces perseverance. Let perseverance finish its work so that you may be mature and complete, not lacking anything."

Prayer:

Father,
When I feel worn out or unseen, remind me You are near. Help me live boldly and obediently, even when it's hard. Mold me, shape me, use this pain for purpose. Strengthen my character in the fire. Thank You for never wasting my suffering and for the promise of eternal

reward. I trust the testing
because I trust *You*.
In Jesus' name,
Amen.

Day 19 – Trust Without a Map

Father, I trust You.
I don't even know the plan —
I see You though, carrying me,
holding my hand.

The unknown, the fear — cast
away when I surrender.
Call You by name — You're
always near,
Making a way, showing Your
face,
The angels in the wind,

All-consuming fire,
I feel You every step, lifting me
higher.

My Father, my God,
In Your peaceful love —

My Lord,
Thank You for saving me
And watching from heaven
above.

Meditation:

It's easy to say "I trust You, God"
when life is predictable. But
when the map disappears, when
we feel surrounded by fog and
fear, that's where real trust
begins. This poem paints a real
picture of what it means to *feel*
God even when we don't
understand God. When we let go
of needing all the answers, we
find His hand already holding
ours. He doesn't just lead from a
distance — He walks with us.
Through fire, through fear, and
into freedom. Faith is less about

knowing the plan and more about knowing *who* holds the plan.

Scripture:

📖 **Psalm 56:3-4 (NIV)**

"When I am afraid, I put my trust in You. In God, whose word I praise—in God I trust and am not afraid."

Prayer:

Yahweh Nissi,
I don't know what's coming ahead — but I know You're with me in it.
When fear rises, let surrender rise higher.

When the way seems unclear, let me feel Your hand in mine.
Help me to trust without seeing,
To walk even when I don't understand it at all,
And to thank You not just for where You're taking me —
But for walking it with me.
Thank You for pouring down blessings in this season, even when it's hard I feel Your grace in every step.
Yahweh Shamma,
Amen.

Day 20 Step Out of the Boat

To jump into Your plan, God, I
want to soar.
If the parachute never opens
from fear, I'll never be in the
place You called me to be.
Father, open the door; restore
the faith.
Let the imagination lead me to
the day where I lay it down — my
way no more.

Soar in Your promises, live in
Your peace, ready to dive in —
You're all I'll ever need. My
everything.
Help me answer the call, the gift
You gave me to set me free.
Father, help me to jump, leave
behind all that's not for me,

Live in Your promises, be all You called me to be.

Meditation:

There comes a moment when standing on the edge is no longer an option. You've prayed. You've planned. You've hesitated. But the change you long for, the destiny God designed for you, is on the other side of the leap. Fear will whisper that the parachute might fail, but faith answers, *"It will not open until I jump."*

Today, imagine what it would look like if you truly surrendered your way for His. Picture yourself soaring above the weight of the past, drifting in peace that only comes from God's promises. This is not a reckless leap — it's a trust fall into the arms of the One who cannot fail.

Scripture:

📖 **Proverbs 3:5-6 (ESV)**

"Trust in the Lord with all your heart, and do not lean on your own understanding. In all your ways acknowledge Him, and He will make straight your paths."

Prayer:

Father God,
I am ready to jump into the plan
You have for me. I want to dive
deep into the heavenly kingdom.
I lay down my fear, my control,
my way of doing things, and I
trust You. I trust what You have
in store for me. Open the door.
You have prepared, restore my
faith where it has been worn
down, and lead me to soar in
what You have prepared for me.
Remove everything in my life
that is not for me and fill me with
courage to step into all You have
called me to be. Today, I choose
faith over fear. I choose the leap.
I choose to dive. Give me eyes to
see You.
In Jesus' name, Amen.

Day 21 Yahweh, You Move in Every Season

You changed every season in my
life.
Lost everything more than twice
—

You gave it back, all tenfold.

Every time I suffered, You held
me so close.
You were near me in every time
of trouble,
Working it for my good.

My Father, my peace, calling me
home,
Molding and restoring me.
Even in the grand plan I can't
see,
I know it's for Your glory.

I've seen You make a miracle out
of me.
You made a way then, and You'll
make a way now.
I'll keep following; I'll let You
lead me.

Trusting all I've already seen,
You set me free from chains that
once held me.
You did it then — You're doing it
now.

The beauty of seeing You move a
mountain,
Seeing You work it all out.

Meditation:

When you look back over your
life, there are seasons that

seemed impossible to survive —
yet here you are. God was
working even when you couldn't
see it. He restored what was lost,
often beyond what you imagined.
And in every trial, His presence
was constant, shaping you into
who you are today.

This truth is the anchor: *If He
did it before, He will do it again.*
The same God who held you in
the valley will guide you on the
mountaintop. The same God who
broke your chains will keep you
free. Trusting His past
faithfulness gives you the
courage to walk boldly into your
future, knowing He's already
gone ahead of you.

Scripture:

📖 **Hebrews 13:8**

"Jesus Christ is the same yesterday and today and forever."

Prayer:

Father God,
Thank You for changing the seasons in my life and for restoring what I thought was gone forever. Thank You for holding me in my darkest moments and turning every trial into something for my good. I trust You because I have seen You move before, and I believe You will move again. Lead me in

the path You have for me. Keep me close, keep me free, and keep me walking in Your promises. In the mighty name of Jesus, Amen.

Day 22 Modern Day David

The words You're calling me to
write; I feel it in my soul.
It's all You in me, by my side, the
Holy Spirit here in the words.
It shines so bright, pouring out
modern day psalms,
Holding me tight, days and
nights.

It takes away the pain, even
restores my faith.
I smile, knowing You have a plan
with this,
Seeing Your grace, pouring out
Your glory in every single page.

All for You — help me stay out of
the way.

Meditation:

When God calls you to create, it's the talent He blesses you with — it's a divine assignment. The words, ideas, and inspiration you feel in your spirit are not from your own strength but from the Holy Spirit at work in you. When we allow Him to guide our pen, our voice, or our art, His glory shines through in ways we could never accomplish on our own.

Staying "out of the way" doesn't mean doing nothing — it means surrendering your pride, control, and fear so that God's Spirit can work without resistance. The most powerful works often come when we stop striving to impress and simply let His presence speak through us.

Scripture:

📖 **Psalm 45:1 (NASB)**

"My heart overflows with a good theme; I address my verses to the King; my tongue is like the pen of a ready scribe."

Prayer:

Father,
Thank You for the words You place in my heart. Thank You for the Holy Spirit that guides my thoughts, inspires my creativity, and turns my pain into praise. Let every word I write and every page I fill be for Your glory alone. Keep me humble. Keep me surrendered. Help me to stay out

of the way so You can move
through me.
In Jesus' name, Amen.

Day 23 Refuge in Your Wings

You are my stronghold in days of
trouble
I will take refuge in the wings of
my Father,
Weeping may come in the night
But I will take joy in You who
never leaves my side,
The world will cause me great
trouble
But You are my comfort in whom
shall I hide,
I delight in Your words for that's
where I find life.

Meditation:

Even in the darkest nights or
most chaotic days, God is your

refuge. His presence surrounds you, His angels are with you, and He knows your heart. He knows your whole soul. Trusting Him doesn't remove all troubles, but it gives you a place of strength and peace amidst them.

Scripture:

📖 **Nahum 1:7**

"The Lord is good, a stronghold in the day of trouble; he knows those who take refuge in him."

Prayer:

Father God,
Thank You that You are my stronghold. When life presses in and sorrow comes, help me to take refuge in Your presence. Teach me to find joy in You even in difficult moments and study Your words that bring life. Surround me with that peace that surpasses all understanding and let me rest in Your love.
In Your loving arms, Amen.

Day 24 The Light of the World

Sitting in the dark right now, my
God is my light.
I'm down, but I'm not out — He's
never lost a fight.

Enemy's crow over me; still not a
shadow of a doubt.
I've seen Him do it before — He'll
keep working it all out.

Show me His ways. I stand in
awe; I stand amazed.
The God, the Father, I give You
all the praise.

Meditation:

Even in the darkest rooms of life,
the presence of God can light

every corner of our heart & soul. We may feel pressed down, worn thin, or surrounded by enemies on every side, but we know the truth — our God has never lost a battle. When we choose hope over defeat, praise over sorrow, we open our eyes to His miracles unfolding even when we can't see the big picture yet.

The enemy may try to magnify the shadows, but the Light of the world cannot be dimmed. Today, instead of focusing on the darkness, let's lean into the truth that God's record is flawless. His faithfulness is unchanging, His light never fails, His hope never goes out.

Scripture:

📖 **Micah 7:8 (NIV)**

"Do not gloat over me, my enemy! Though I have fallen, I will rise. Though I sit in darkness, the Lord will be my light."

Prayer:

Yahweh, My Redeemer,
You are my hope. Father, I will praise You in every storm. In moments when I feel surrounded and the shadows seem to close in, help me remember that You are my light. You have never lost a fight, nor will You ever lose the battle. When the enemy tries to talk down to me, let Your truth rise louder in my heart & soul

than any lie. I stand in awe of who You are and what You've done. Keep showing me Your ways, Father, and I will keep giving You all the praise. You are the God of angel armies & I praise You again & again.
Amen

Day 25 Seek & You Will Find, Knock & the Door Will Be Opened

I could read a million lines, and I
quote scripture time after time.
If I'm not seeking, I will not find.
Speaking to my Father, I fall
short every time.

Every meditation, yet another
rhyme.
One more meditation — it's a
worldly lie.
It's in His Word; it's in making
the time.

If I'm seeking, I will find,
a God, a Father by my side.
Seeking includes speaking — one
more poem, one more cry.

Meditation:

Sometimes we fill our days with words, prayers, and even scripture, yet our hearts still feel far away. True seeking isn't about how much we read it's about intentionally drawing close to God with an open heart. He promises that if we seek Him, we *will* find Him. Today, I challenge you to get on your knees & talk to your heavenly Father.

Scripture:

📖 **Jeremiah 29:13**

"You will seek me and find me when you seek me with all your heart."

Prayer:

Father God,
I don't want to just go through the motions. Teach me to truly seek You, not only with words but with my heart. Thank You for always being by my side, even when I fall short. I want to stay in Your Word. I want to know You so deeply & closely Father. Draw me closer to You each day and let my seeking lead me deeper into Your presence.
Amen.

Day 26 Beauty from Ashes

You restore what this life has broken.
Keep it simple, staying still, praising Your name, Father, Your will.
I pray for Your wisdom. I thank You for using me, even though I got faith of a mustard seed.
I am the vessel that sets the captives free.
You are so worthy. I've been redeemed.
Father, I love You.
You set me free, Yahweh.
When I got nothing, You still speak through me.

Meditation:

From dust we were created, and to dust we will return. (Genesis 3:19) Yet in between those ashes, God breathes His Spirit into us. Our brokenness does not disqualify us—it becomes the place where His glory shines brightest. When life leaves us shattered, He restores. When we feel unworthy, He still speaks through us. Even faith as small as a mustard seed can be enough for Him to move mountains.

Scripture:

📖 **Isaiah 61:3**

"He gives beauty for ashes, the oil of joy for mourning, the garment of praise for the spirit of heaviness; that they may be called trees of righteousness, the planting of the Lord, that He may be glorified."

Prayer:

Father God,
I lay my ashes before You, trusting that You will bring beauty from them. Thank You for restoring what life has broken and for speaking through me, even when I feel weak and unworthy. Breathe new life into every place of mourning,

heaviness, and emptiness. Let my mustard seed of faith grow into a testimony of Your power. I give You glory, Yahweh.

Amen.

Day 27: Holy Spirit Surprise

Here I stand—on holy ground.
Roots run deep, no longer bound,
chains are breaking,
We sing, we shout, we praise—
We go up to the altar
We make your bed, knowing you
will leave
with something you never knew.
A Holy Spirit surprise
Waiting just for you.
The light's so bright,
the quiet time—just on time.
Don't anticipate—
God works in His own rhyme.
The place is sacred—take your
time.
Lay it all at the foot of that cross
Tears flow deep as you read
every letter, every line.

You'll know this was
orchestrated—
way before your time.
You'll know a light,
you'll see His love—
AGAPE, AGAPE—
Heaven above,
the light of Jesus in the world.
A new disciple, bold.
A new warrior for You,
wrapped in armor.
The battle will wait.
Quote Ephesians—
Keep praying it away.
God's not left you—
but now you're so close,
the enemy will come,
Try knocking at your door.
He has no power to the divine.
I don't want you to fall
for a single trap in the lie.
You've found the grace—

you've won a gift
in a holy place.
The way to keep it
is to continue
in that secret escape.

Meditation:

God's presence often surprises us
in the quiet moments and in the
crowded altar calls. What feels
like chance is His orchestration -
planned long before our time.
The "Holy Spirit surprise" is the
reminder that chains really are
breaking, and that His love—
agape love—covers us fully.

Spiritual battles may follow
mountaintop moments, but we
are not left unarmed. The armor
of God is our daily covering, and

prayer is our weapon. When chills run through your soul, it's His Spirit testifying that you are not only redeemed but also called, chosen, and equipped for the fight.

Scripture:

📖 **Ephesians 6:13**

"Therefore, put on the full armor of God, so that when the day of evil comes, you may be able to stand your ground, and after you have done everything, to stand."

Prayer:

Father,
Thank You for the surprise of Your Spirit, for the moments where chains fall, and Your light shines brighter than anything around me. Teach me to take my time in Your presence, to lay everything at the cross, and to trust that You have orchestrated my steps long before I walked them. Clothe me in Your armor and keep me steadfast in prayer that I may stand against every lie of the enemy. Fill me with boldness as Your disciple and warrior.
In Jesus' name, Amen.

Day 28 –Meet Him at the Crossroads

You are a refuge in the dead of night even at the crossroads. I know You will still shine light, in the depths of my soul I know You hold me close. A good Father never let's go.

Meditation:

Life beats us down sometimes, reminds us we are just a grain of sand —ashes to ashes, dust to dust. Even in the darkest hours, God is in it with you fighting for you. He is our refuge, the never-failing light at the crossroads, the hand that will never let us fall. Even when everything feels like it's falling apart on every single side, He holds us close. His love is unshakable, His presence is unmovable, and His promises unbreakable. Nothing can separate us from the love of God (including us).

Scripture:

📖 **Mattew 7:14**

But small is the gate and narrow the road that leads to life, and only a few find it."

Prayer:

Yahweh, I am tired, Father, I feel every weakness today. Remind me, Father, You are my strength. You are the Good Shepherd.

Thanks for holding me when the night is a heavy burden and the way is so unclear. Help me surrender and trust You. You shine bright lights out of the darkest paths. Help me to hold on to the miracles You perform. Father, I trust You even here, God. I believe You work it out for my good. You never let me go. May I pick up my cross completely and follow You.
In the mighty name of Jesus,
Amen.

Day 29 - The Father's Call

You call me out, call me still
Scary and full of fear, out of the
comfort zone,
Every prayer I prayed, You hear
every word,
The call to grace I can't dismiss,
the complacency a slow abyss,
I prayed for eyes to see,
I told You, Father, to not let me
miss the call You had for me
I see it clear, it's in my touch,
Every mountain I had to climb
was for this very moment
the exciting rush to see You build
me in the climb
 to know my Father is always on
time.

Meditation:

When God calls us out of our comfort zone, it's rarely calm or convenient — it's holy. The climb is where we're built, where we find out that every unanswered prayer was really an invitation to trust deeper. The rush of fear turns into awe when we realize God has been shaping our steps all along. Today, rest in the truth that the call on your life is *on purpose* and *on time.*

Scripture:

📖 **1 Thessalonians 5:24 (NIV)**

"The one who calls you is faithful, and he will do it."

📖 Psalm 18:33 31:8 (NIV)

"He makes my feet like the feet of a deer; he causes me to stand on the heights."

Prayer:

Father, thank You for calling me out and calling me still. Even when fear grips me, I know You are guiding each step. Open my eyes wider to see Your hand in the climb and help me trust that every mountain has meaning. Remove complacency from my spirit and replace it with courage, faith, and readiness. Let every prayer I pray rise as a reminder that You hear me, and You are faithful to finish what You began. In Jesus' name, Amen.

Day 30- The Father's Phoenix

I sat through seasons of
desperation,
and not once did You not come
through.
You showed me, each time and
each line,
every rhyme, that You make all
things new.

You healed my heart and cleared
every wreckage from my past.
I was once nothing other than
shattered glass.
I cut, and I made people bleed—
but then my Father, God, came
and rescued me.

You turned it around, all put
back together now.

Not only that—You work through
me to make other glass whole.
I am Your clay; You are the mold.

I was the lost sheep, and You left
the ninety-nine.
You rejoice in my presence
and then helped me to save the
same kind.

I am grateful, I am whole—
Jesus Christ, You saved my soul.
Now use me to bring the light,
I can see it all so clear:
You always had me in Your
sights,
turning ashes into beauty,
knowing someday that I'd answer
the call.

Showing Your glory, saving the
broken when they fall—
it's Your story, not mine at all.

Jesus Christ, the same yesterday
and tomorrow,
the same God who had Moses
flee
is the same God that rescues you
and me.

If you are in the pit, don't lose
hope.
Yahweh, my God, can redeem.

Just surrender.
Let go.

Meditation:

Life has seasons of breaking and
seasons of mending. What once
was ashes, God breathes into
beauty. What once was death,
Christ raises into life. The same
God who split the sea, shut the
mouths of lions, and gave

strength to the weak is still faithful right here in the now. Hebrews tells us of a great cloud of witnesses who walked by faith, not by sight, enduring trials, hardships, and suffering—yet they kept their eyes fixed on the promise, on His promise.

Faith is not about never facing fire; it's about trusting God in the middle of it. Every trial, every setback, every tear has a purpose in the hands of the Redeemer. He calls us not only to survive but to *run the race* set before us with endurance. Are you running with your eyes fixed on Jesus? Because in Him, ashes become beauty, brokenness becomes wholeness, and death gives way to life.

Scripture:

📖 **Hebrews 12:1-2**

"Therefore, since we are surrounded by so great a cloud of witnesses, let us also lay aside every weight, and sin which clings so closely, and let us run with endurance the race that is set before us, looking to Jesus, the founder and perfecter of our faith, who for the joy that was set before him endured the cross, despising the shame, and is seated at the right hand of the throne of God."

Prayer:

Father,
Thank You for being the God
who turns ashes into beauty,

death into life, and brokenness into healing. Just as You strengthened the heroes of faith in Hebrews, strengthen me to walk by faith and not by sight. Help me lay down every weight that slows me, every fear that binds me, and run the race You've set before me with endurance. Thank You that my trials are not wasted and that my life has purpose in Your hands. I surrender all—let Your story be told through me.

In Jesus' name, Amen.

Final Reflection

Thank you for reading my personal cries to God. I hope it helped you feel closer to His presence. I hope it brought some purpose, some peace, and days of growth in your life.

I don't know your journey or the burdens you carry, but I do know that when I take mine to Jesus and spend quiet time with God, I am lighter. I am free. I have peace. That is my wish for you, dear reader — that you don't let this world mold you with its social media and all its schemes to pull you away from a peaceful, still moment with Him.

Maybe your quiet place is in nature, on your back porch

swing, or in that rocking chair in the front yard. Maybe it's stepping out of your office into that alone spot, the back of a rehab smoke deck, or that pantry in the sober living house that no one comes into. Wherever your quiet moment is, I hope you are having that moment with our Creator.

I hope you have His peace, and that you have given Him your heart. And if you haven't, I pray right now that you just say these simple words:

"Jesus, I am a sinner. Please come into my heart as my Lord and my Savior."

I attend a church full of broken people who just want to be better. Bring your brokenness to

God — whether in church or in a quiet time — get in His Word and find the peace that surpasses all understanding, hope in chaos.

Thank you for going on this journey with me.
I hope to write again soon.

Love,

Ashley Arendale Murphy

www.ingramcontent.com/pod-product-compliance
Lightning Source LLC
Chambersburg PA
CBHW071750120626
46550CB00002B/741